Written by Jenny White
Illustrated by Antjuan Goodwin

Junior Rabbit Travels to New York
Copyright © 2024 by Jenny O. White. All rights reserved.

No part of this publication may be reproduced, stored in a retrieval system or transmitted in any way by any means, electronic, mechanical, photocopy, recording or otherwise without the prior permission of the author except as provided by USA copyright law.

The opinions expressed by the author are not necessarily those of Stonehenge Literary and Media.

1846 E Innovation Park Dr STE 100 Oro Valley, AZ 85755

Veritas Ink and Press is committed to excellence in the publishing Industry.

Book Design copyright 2023 by Veritas Ink and Press. All rights Reserved.

Published in the United States of America

ISBN: 979-8-8693-6534-7
eISBN: 979-8-8693-6535-4

Junior Rabbit Travels to New York

ENTRANCE
PSSST! Junior,
OVER HERE!

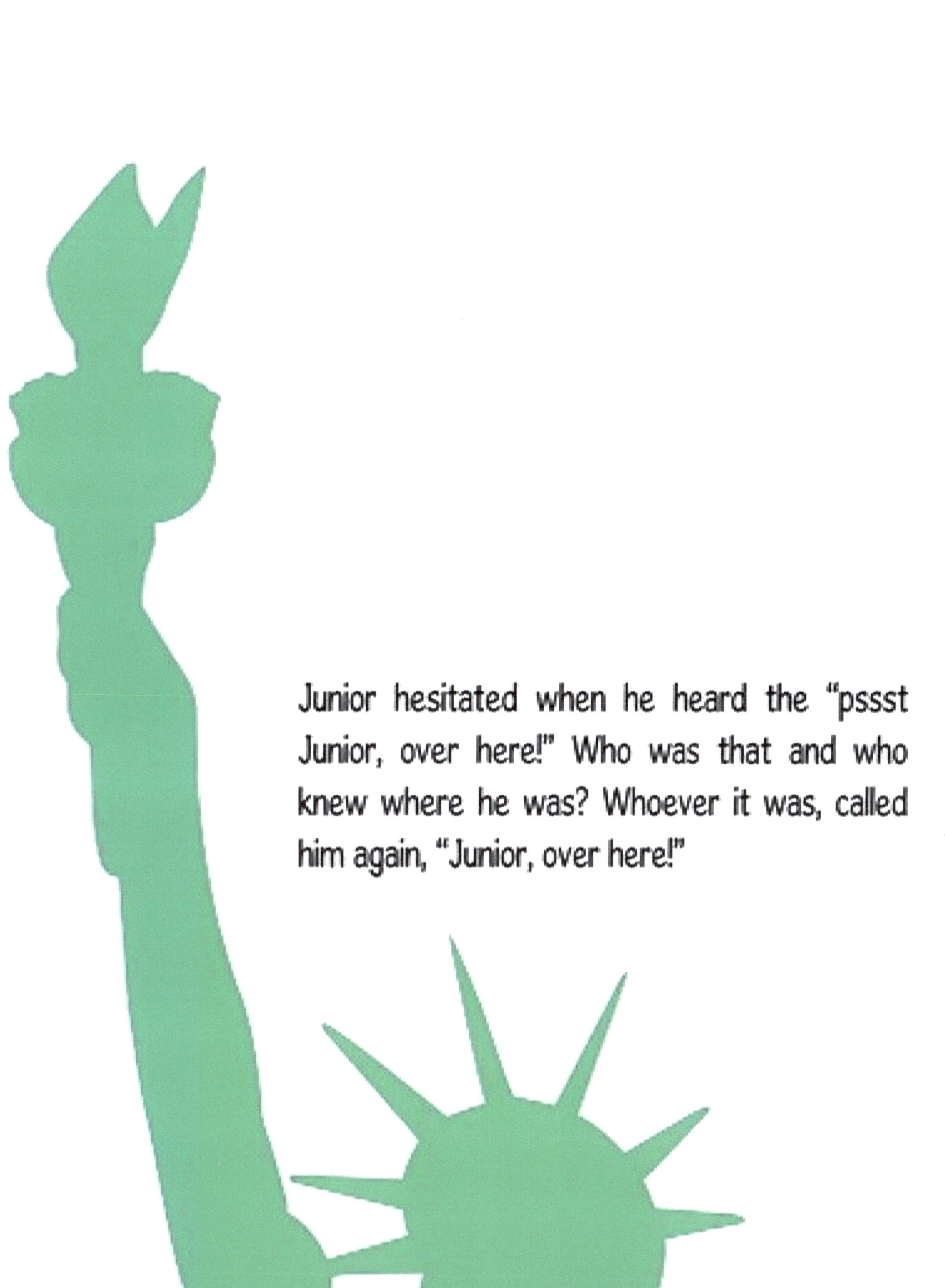

Junior hesitated when he heard the "pssst Junior, over here!" Who was that and who knew where he was? Whoever it was, called him again, "Junior, over here!"

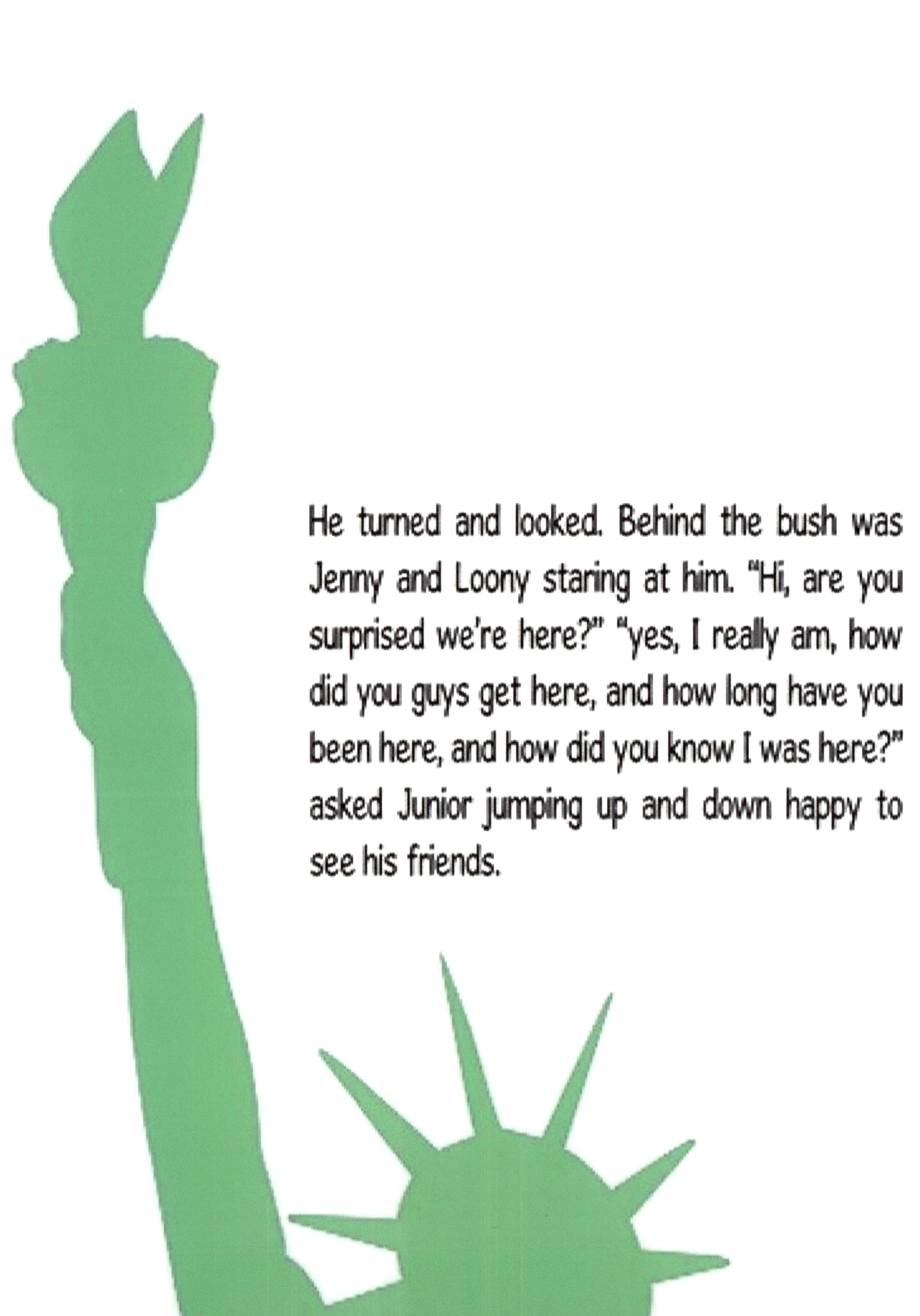

He turned and looked. Behind the bush was Jenny and Loony staring at him. "Hi, are you surprised we're here?" "yes, I really am, how did you guys get here, and how long have you been here, and how did you know I was here?" asked Junior jumping up and down happy to see his friends.

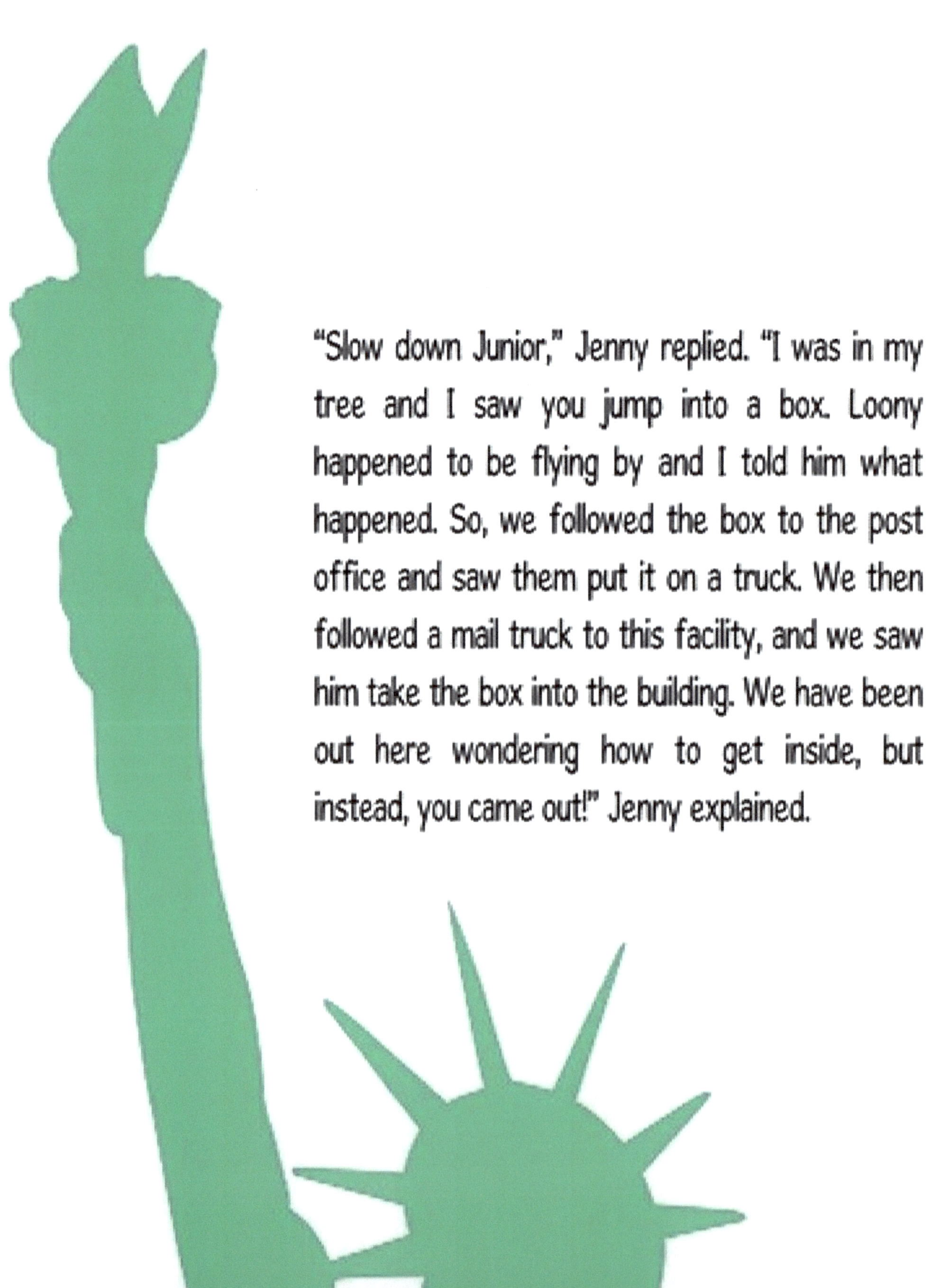

"Slow down Junior," Jenny replied. "I was in my tree and I saw you jump into a box. Loony happened to be flying by and I told him what happened. So, we followed the box to the post office and saw them put it on a truck. We then followed a mail truck to this facility, and we saw him take the box into the building. We have been out here wondering how to get inside, but instead, you came out!" Jenny explained.

MAIL

"Wow guys, you've been on a real trip!" Junior said. "So, have you," Loony chimed in. "How was it?" "Scary," Junior answered without hesitation, "Let's get out of here and go home."

ENTRANCE

So, Junior got on Loony's back and Jenny did too and they began their flight back home.

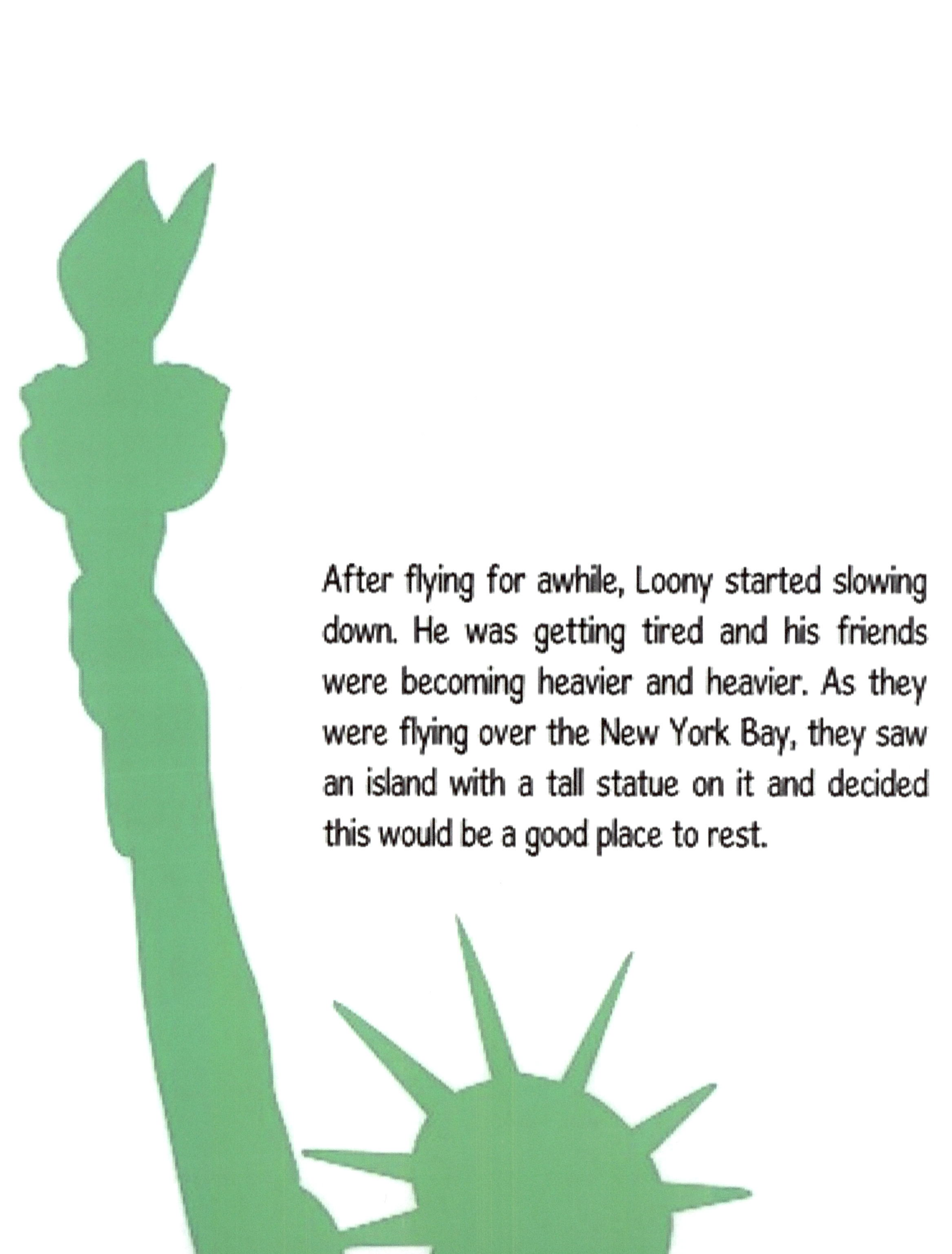

After flying for awhile, Loony started slowing down. He was getting tired and his friends were becoming heavier and heavier. As they were flying over the New York Bay, they saw an island with a tall statue on it and decided this would be a good place to rest.

Can you guess what the statue was boys and girls? Yes, it was the Statue of Liberty standing proud on Liberty Island. They soon found a spot to land, behind a tree near the statue.

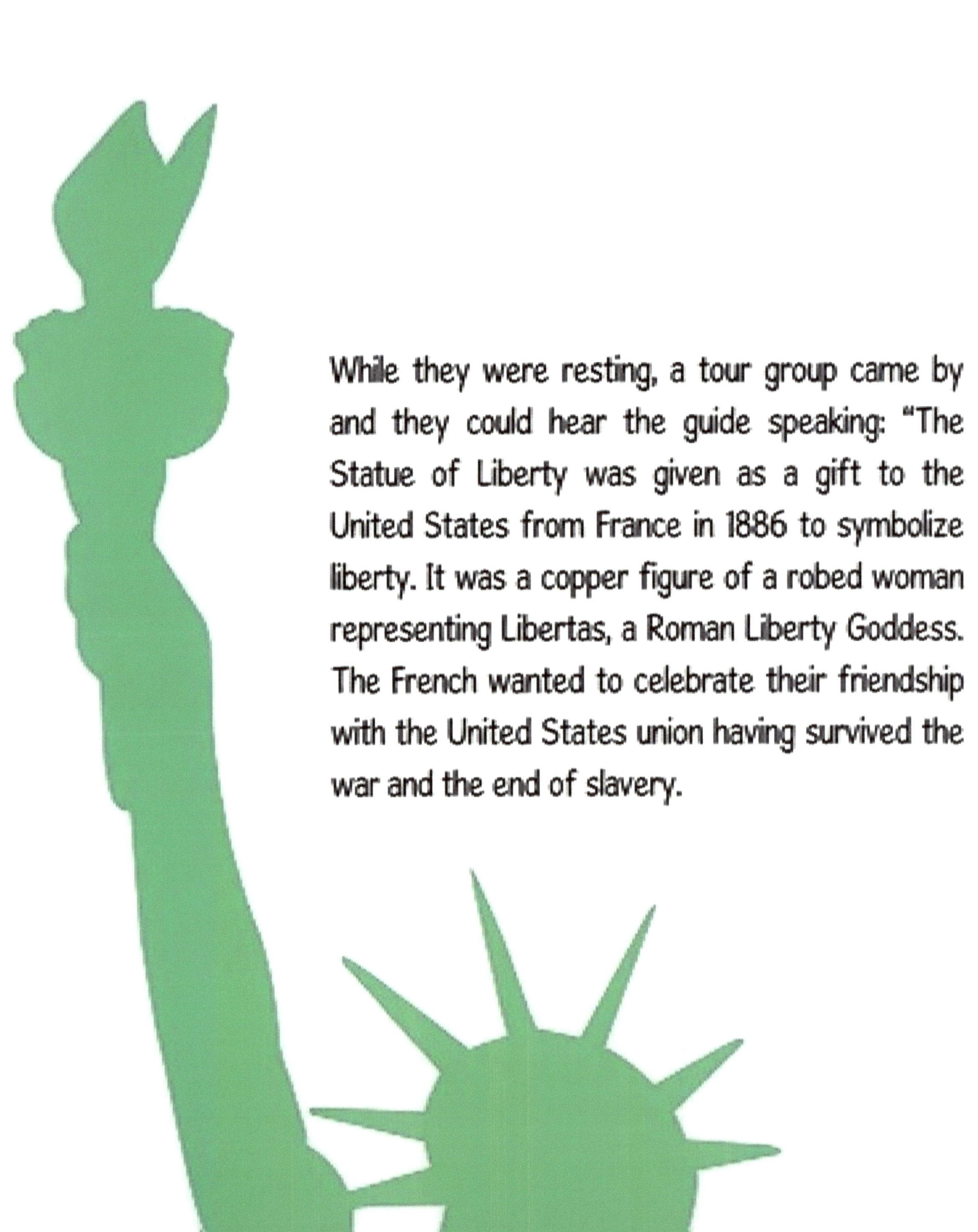

While they were resting, a tour group came by and they could hear the guide speaking: "The Statue of Liberty was given as a gift to the United States from France in 1886 to symbolize liberty. It was a copper figure of a robed woman representing Libertas, a Roman Liberty Goddess. The French wanted to celebrate their friendship with the United States union having survived the war and the end of slavery.

In her left hand she carries a tablet of the law marked with the date of the Declaration of Independence;

JULY
IV
MDCCLXXVI

in her right hand she raises a torch of enlightenment

and with her left foot she tramples a broken chain symbolizing the end of slavery.

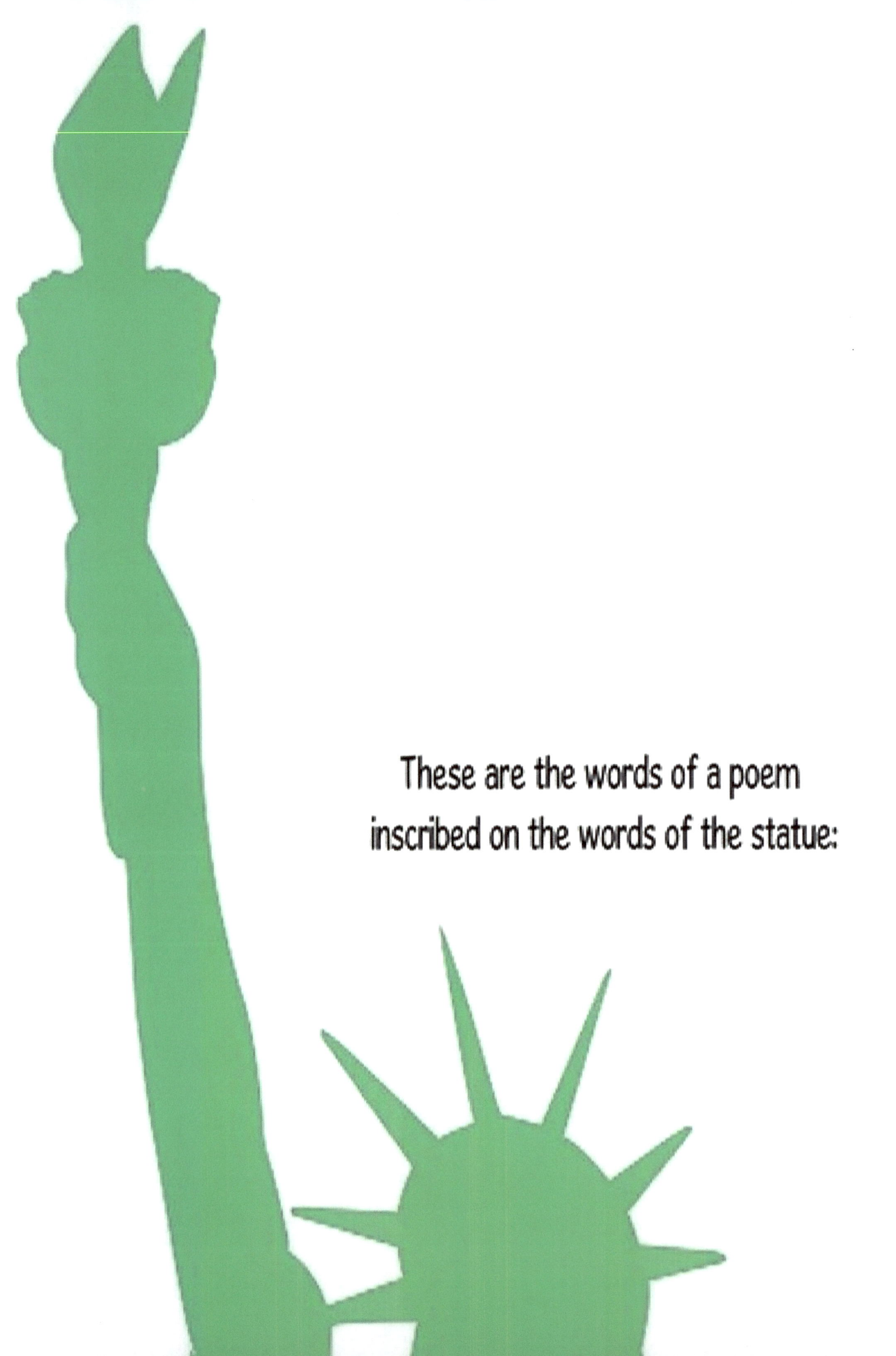

These are the words of a poem
inscribed on the words of the statue:

New Colossus

Not like the brazen giant of Greek fame,

With conquering limbs astride from land to land;

Here at our sea-washed, sunset gates shall stand

A mighty woman with a torch, whose flame

Is the imprisoned lightning, and her name

Mother of Exiles. From her beacon-hand

Glows world-wide welcome; her mild eyes command

The air-bridged harbor that twin cities frame.

"Keep, ancient lands, your storied pomp!" cries she

With silent lips. "Give me your tired, your poor,

Your huddled masses yearning to breathe free,

The wretched refuse of your teeming shore.

Send these, the homeless, tempest-tossed to me,

I lift my lamp beside the golden door!"

Emma Lazarus

(11-02-1883)

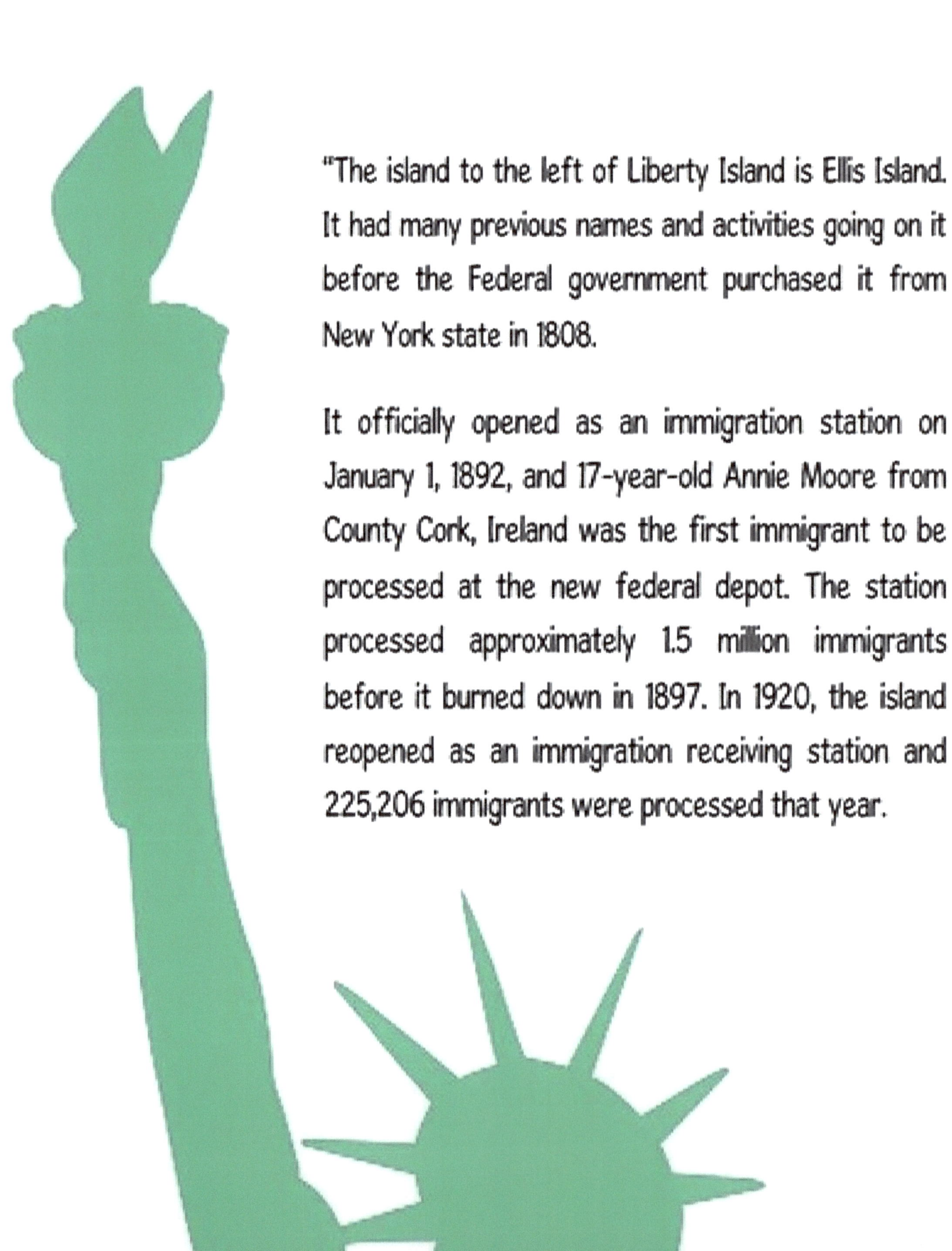

"The island to the left of Liberty Island is Ellis Island. It had many previous names and activities going on it before the Federal government purchased it from New York state in 1808.

It officially opened as an immigration station on January 1, 1892, and 17-year-old Annie Moore from County Cork, Ireland was the first immigrant to be processed at the new federal depot. The station processed approximately 1.5 million immigrants before it burned down in 1897. In 1920, the island reopened as an immigration receiving station and 225,206 immigrants were processed that year.

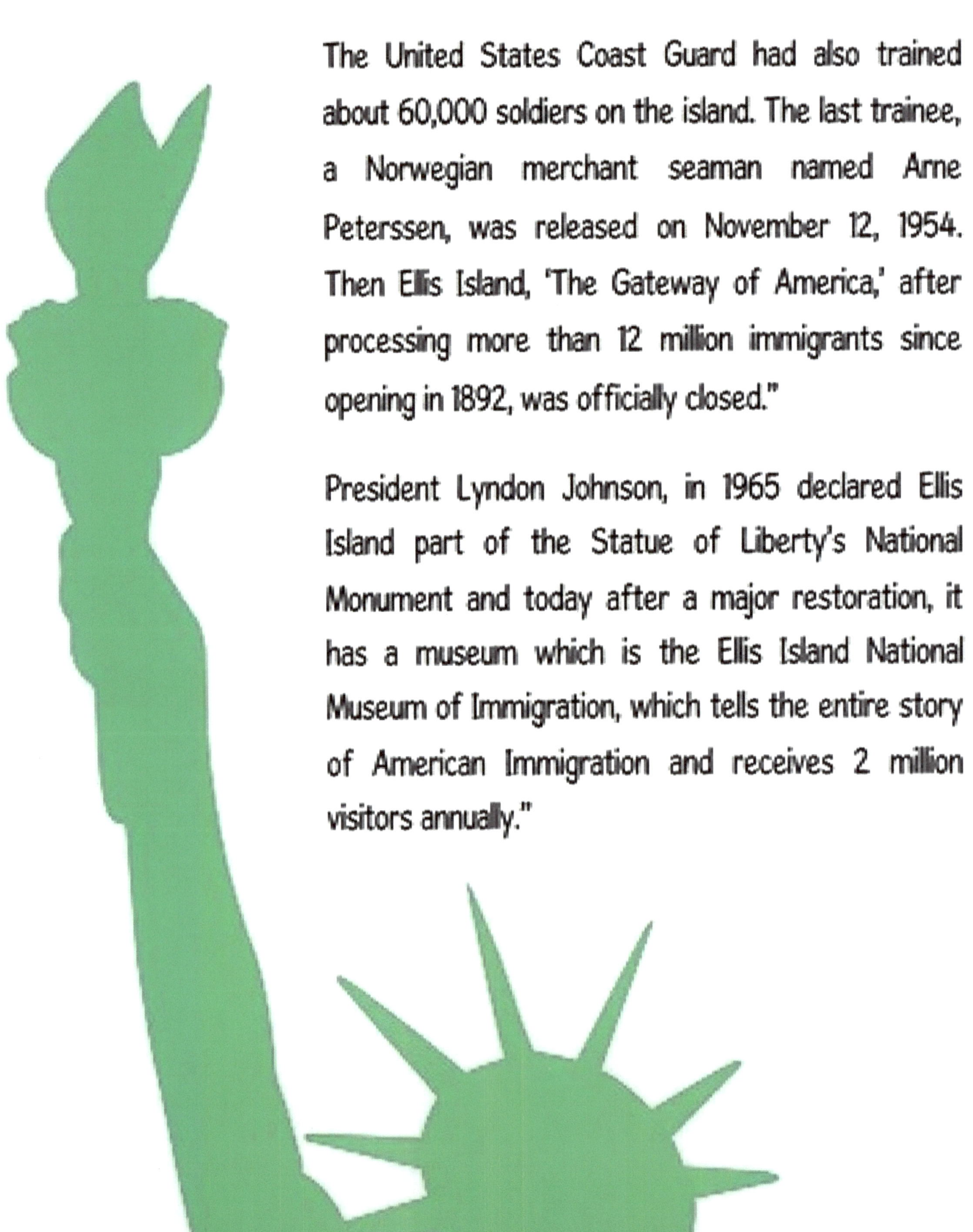

The United States Coast Guard had also trained about 60,000 soldiers on the island. The last trainee, a Norwegian merchant seaman named Arne Peterssen, was released on November 12, 1954. Then Ellis Island, 'The Gateway of America,' after processing more than 12 million immigrants since opening in 1892, was officially closed."

President Lyndon Johnson, in 1965 declared Ellis Island part of the Statue of Liberty's National Monument and today after a major restoration, it has a museum which is the Ellis Island National Museum of Immigration, which tells the entire story of American Immigration and receives 2 million visitors annually."

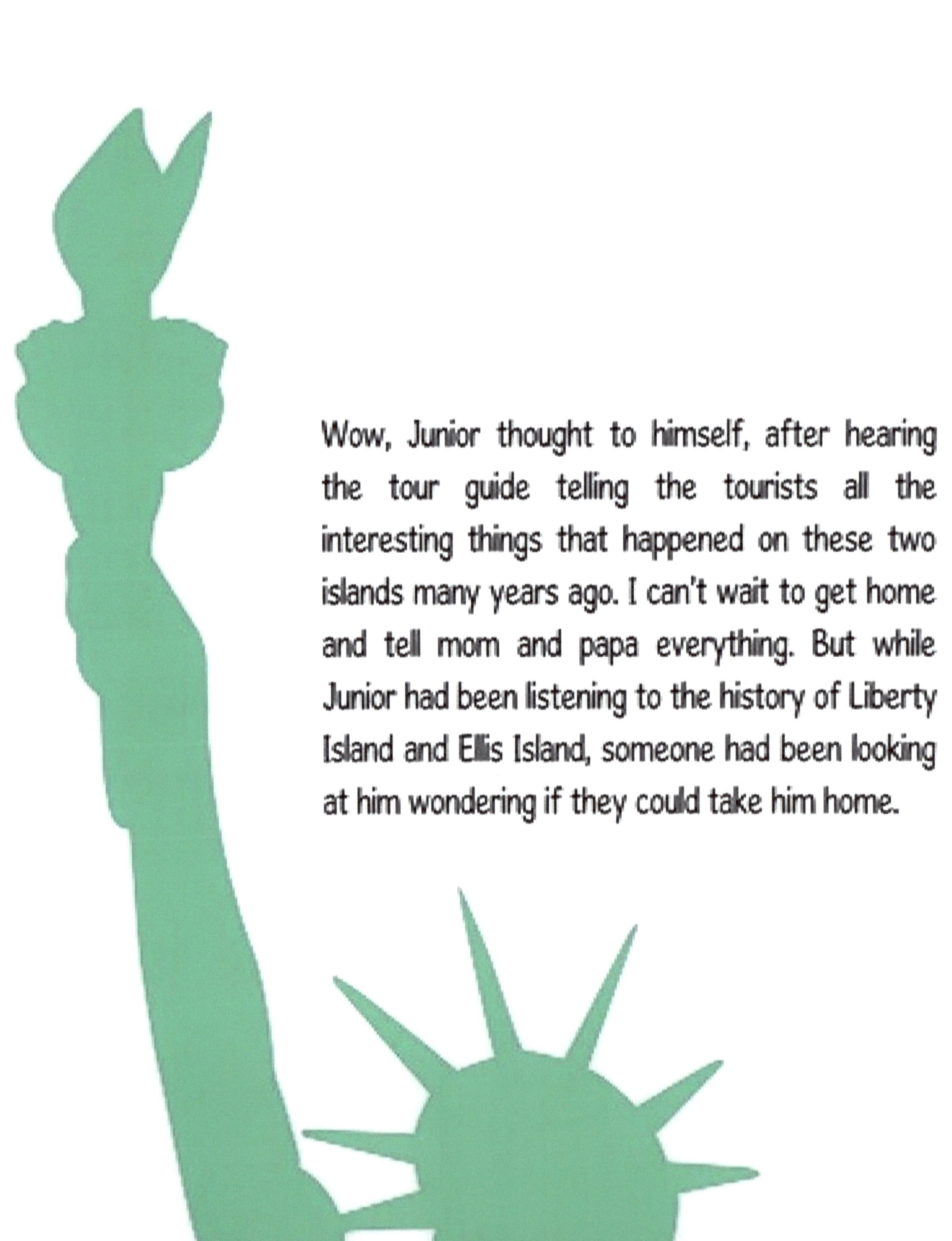

Wow, Junior thought to himself, after hearing the tour guide telling the tourists all the interesting things that happened on these two islands many years ago. I can't wait to get home and tell mom and papa everything. But while Junior had been listening to the history of Liberty Island and Ellis Island, someone had been looking at him wondering if they could take him home.

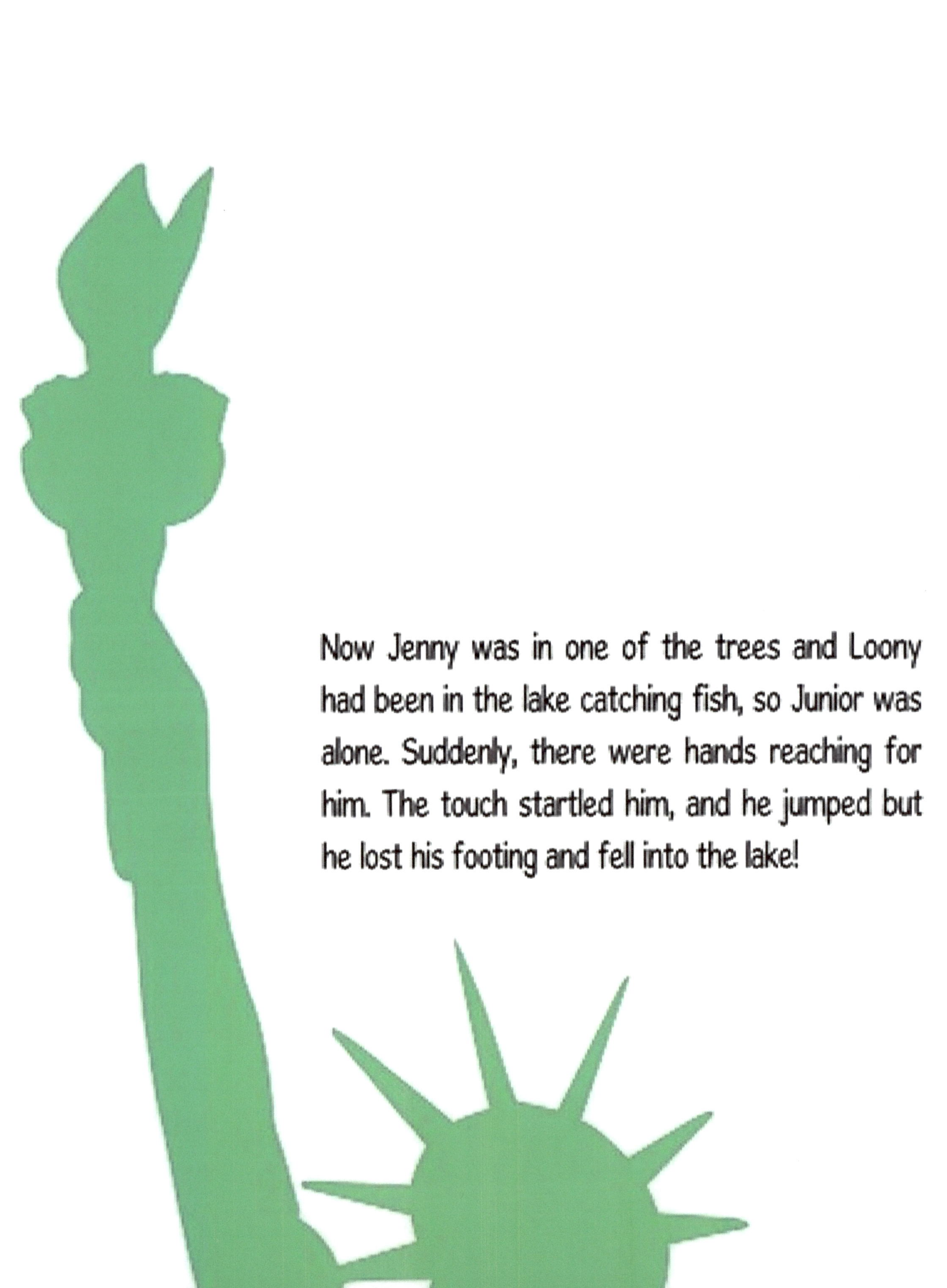

Now Jenny was in one of the trees and Loony had been in the lake catching fish, so Junior was alone. Suddenly, there were hands reaching for him. The touch startled him, and he jumped but he lost his footing and fell into the lake!

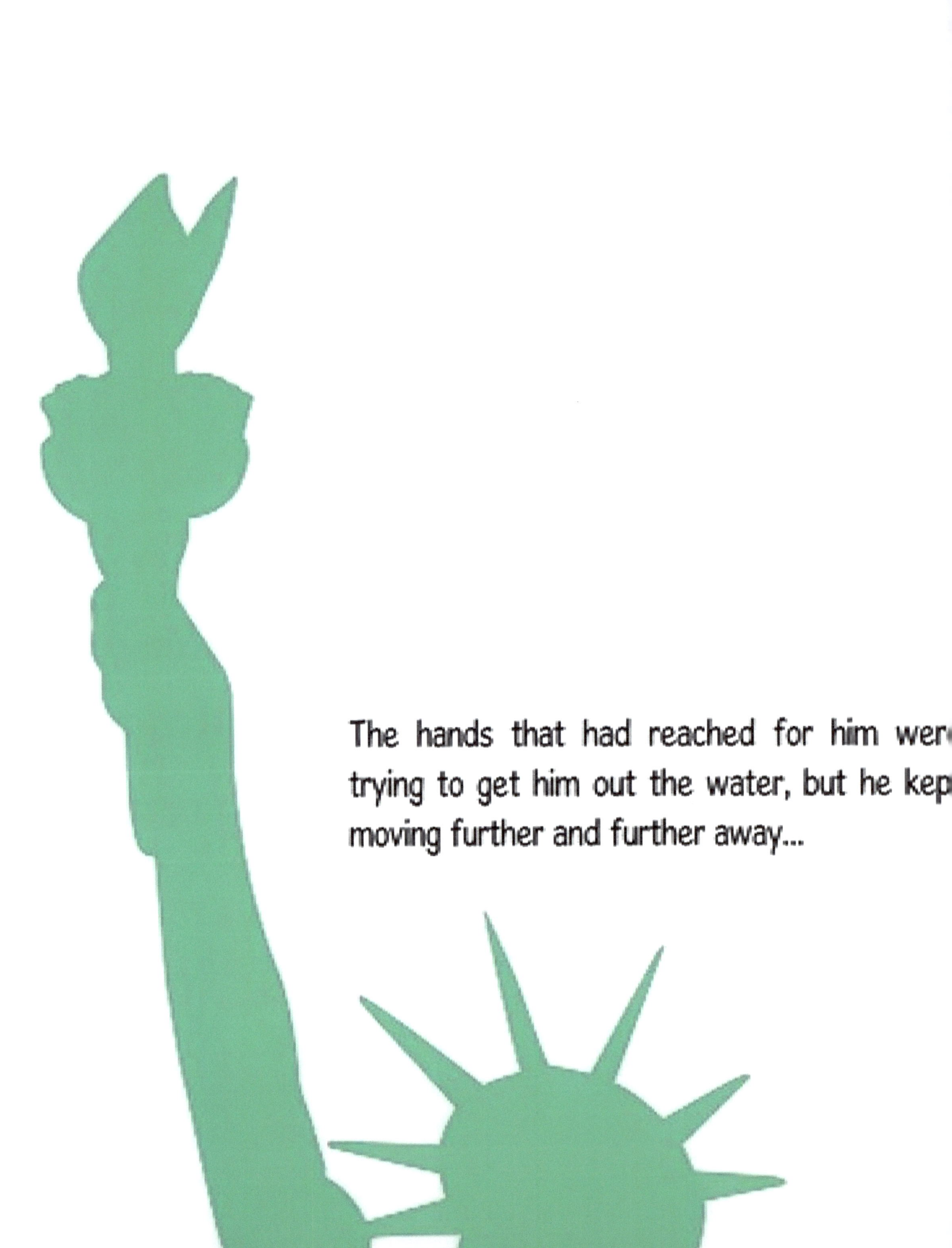

The hands that had reached for him were trying to get him out the water, but he kept moving further and further away...

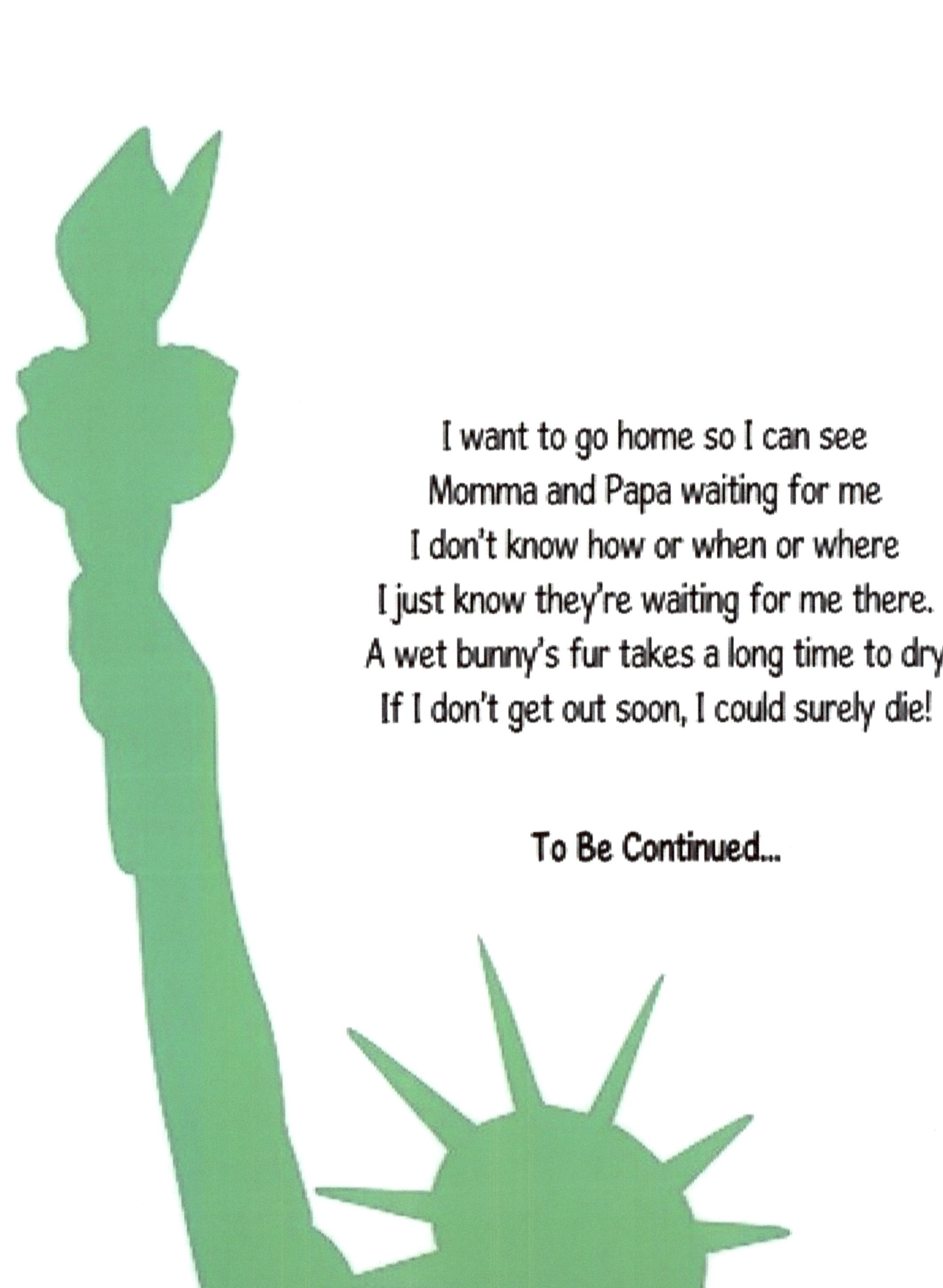

I want to go home so I can see
Momma and Papa waiting for me
I don't know how or when or where
I just know they're waiting for me there.
A wet bunny's fur takes a long time to dry
If I don't get out soon, I could surely die!

To Be Continued...

87
81
SARATOGA SPRINGS
ROCHESTER
SYRACUSE
ALBANY
BUFFALO
90
New York
THE EMPIRE STATE
NEW YORK CITY